King Canute
and the tide

Story written by Adrian Bradbury
Illustrated by Tim Archbold

Speed Sounds

Consonants *Ask children to say the sounds.*

f	l	m	n	r	s	v	z	sh	th	ng
ff	ll	mm	nn	rr	ss	ve	zz			nk
ph	(le)	mb	(kn)	wr	se		se			
			gn		c		(s)			
					ce					

b	c	d	g	h	j	p	qu	t	w	x	y	ch
bb	k	dd	gg		g	pp		tt	wh			(tch)
	ck		gu		ge							
					dge							

Each box contains one sound but sometimes more than one grapheme.
*Focus graphemes for this story are **circled**.*

Vowels

Ask children to say the sounds in and out of order.

a	e	i	o	u	ay	ee	igh	ow
	ea				a-e	ea	i-e	o-e
					a	y	ie	o
						e	i	oe
at	hen	in	on	up	day	see	high	blow

oo	oo	ar	or	air	ir	ou	oy
u-e			oor	are	ur	ow	oi
ue			ore		er		
			aw				
zoo	look	car	for	fair	whirl	shout	boy

Story Green Words

Ask children to read the words first in Fred Talk and then say the word.

true   throne   broke   tide   wise   lord   learnt*

Ask children to say the syllables and then read the whole word.

Can|ute   ad|vise   king|dom   batt|le   ma|jes|ty   high|ness
might|y   hon|est*   du|ty*

Ask children to read the root first and then the whole word with the suffix.

rule → ruled   duke → dukes   command → commanded
smile → smiling   bellow → bellowed   continue → continued
lap → lapped   finger → fingers*   flatter → flattering*

* Challenge Words

Vocabulary Check

Discuss the meaning (as used in the story) after the children have read each word.

	definition:	**sentence:**
duty	a job that must be done	It was their duty to advise Canute...
foolish	silly	... each foolish duke just said what they thought the king wanted them to say.
flatter	to say nice things	It became a battle to see who could flatter Canute the most...
mighty	great	"Mighty Canute, when you speak, everyone and everything does as you command!"
command	telling someone what to do	"... everyone and everything does as you command!"
bellowed	shouted	"Tide, I command you to stop!" he bellowed.

Red Words

great	watch	who	how
could	small	over	their
any	thought	people	call
want	come	were	put
my	everyone	there	one

King Canute and the tide

A long, long time ago there lived a wise king called Canute. He ruled his land firmly but fairly. There was just one thing that put him in a bad mood: his dukes.

The dukes were very rich men. It was their duty to advise Canute on how to run his huge kingdom and do the right thing for his people.

But instead of helping the king, each foolish duke just said what they thought the king wanted them to say. It became a battle to see who could flatter Canute the most...

"My lord! You are the greatest king!"
Canute sighed and drummed his fingers.

"Your majesty, the sun, moon and
stars kneel at your feet!"
Canute felt his rage growing.

"Mighty Canute, when you speak,
everyone and everything does as
you command!"
It was no use, Canute couldn't
put up with this anymore.

"Follow me!" Canute commanded. "And bring my throne!"

With that, the king marched across the sand dunes and on to the beach. Canute settled on his throne and watched as the waves lapped in and out, across the sand.

"So, you say I am a mighty king?" Canute asked.
The dukes nodded.

"You say that everything does
as I command?"

"That's true, your highness!"
the dukes agreed.

"Very well, let's see, shall we?"
replied Canute, smiling
to himself.

Lifting his hand, he shouted: "Sea, go back!"
The waves crept up the sand.

"Tide, I command you to stop!" he bellowed.
A small wave broke over his toes. Soon his boots
were wet. Then his ankles.
Then his shins.

Canute rose from his throne and spoke to his dukes: "You see, I am just a man like you," he said. "I cannot control the sea."

"A king's job is difficult," he continued. "You must stop flattering me and start helping me. When you speak, you must be honest and true."

From that day on, the dukes advised the king well. They had learnt an important lesson from wise King Canute.

Questions to talk about

Ask children to TTYP each question using 'Fastest finger' (FF) or 'Have a think' (HaT).

p.9 (HaT) Was King Canute a good king? How do you know?

p.10 (HaT) Did the dukes really mean everything they said to the king?

p.11 (HaT) Which sentence tells us that Canute was becoming angry?

p.12 (FF) What did Canute ask the dukes to bring to the beach?

p.14 (FF) What happened when Canute commanded the waves to go back?

p.14 (HaT) Did Canute expect the tide to stop coming in?

p.15 (HaT) Did Canute's plan work? How do you know?

Questions to read and answer

(Children complete without your help.)

1. King Canute was very **wise / rude / little**.

2. The king's **dukes / land / horses** put him in a bad mood.

3. The dukes' job was to **rule / advise / feed** Canute.

4. King Canute marched across the **sand dunes / forest / kingdom**.

5. The king's boots got **grassy / muddy / wet**.

Speedy Green Words

Ask children to practise reading the words across the rows, down the columns and in and out of order clearly and quickly.

speak	like	each	boots
asked	use	wave	say
shouted	grow	moon	start
fair	right	spoke	huge
toes	soon	feet	rose